Being Calm
Being You

Ian Parks

ISBN:1466387807
ISBN-13:9781466387805

For my parents, thank you

CONTENTS

PREFACE

When I was seventeen years old I suffered my first panic attack. At that time I did not know what I was experiencing was a panic attack. I literally thought I was dying, maybe going mad, or that my head was just about to explode! I was many miles from home, on my own and to make matters really uncomfortable I was in the middle of the Friday evening rush hour on the London Underground. Not exactly the most relaxing place to be at the best of times, but there I was. I had just boarded a London Underground Tube train and the doors had slid closed, right in front of my face.

The train pulled off and began to pick up speed. I began to feel stuck. I was in a crowded carriage full of people and my face was pressed almost against the window. As the train pulled up at the next stop there was the usual pushing and shoving and maneuverings of people trying to get on and off, or even just stay on, the train. After a few minutes I found myself still on the train but turned around so that I was facing into the carriage as the train pulled off again. Right then, for some reason I decided that I had to get off! I just had to! Something wasn't right and I had to get off.

But I couldn't. The next few hours of my life are nothing but a blur to me even today. I have vague memories but nothing I could rely on. However after a few hours, a great deal of tears, anguish and confusion I eventually managed to make it to my destination.

Instead of the relief I had expected and craved, I found myself becoming even more anxious and starting to panic again. I really felt that I wanted to be at home, back in familiar surroundings. Over that weekend I grew more anxious and more fearful every hour. I began to worry about getting back on a train to come home. The worry grew and when it finally came time to return home, instead of being able to get back onto a train to retrace my journey, something that I had done hundreds of times without a thought, I panicked again and fled from the railway station.

I retried a few times but couldn't bring myself to put a foot onto a train carriage. Eventually I called my parents and pleaded with them to drive for over four hours to come and help me. I don't think I'll ever be able to properly thank them for that, what they did for me that day and night felt like some sort of emergency rescue mission to me, but to them it must have seemed like their son had lost his mind, ranting about feeling weird and not being able to get on a train. What must that have sounded like? That desperate phone call from me and their subsequent four hour drive must have left them out of their minds with worry and concern. Kids eh!

But they came.

They brought me home.

For a while I thought my life would return to normal...

Over the following weeks and months I found that panic attacks would occur more frequently. By this time I had discovered that this was what they were called but I was no closer to understanding what they really were. All I knew was that they scared the hell out of me and I wanted nothing more than to never have another one ever again. So I began to arrange my life to avoid being in any situation where I had previously had an attack or where thought I might even be at risk of having one.

I stopped taking the train to work and instead would catch a lift with my father every day. Fortunately he worked in the same town. At this point I still managed to get onto the train for the journey home.

But the attacks continued and I wasn't getting any closer to really understanding what was happening to me, I began to find it harder and harder to face getting on that train home. Eventually even the journey to work in the morning in the relative safety and comfortable surroundings of my father's car became more of an issue until eventually I swallowed my pride and went to talk to a Counsellor about what was actually happening to me.

I was really unlucky with my first choice of Counsellor. His advice was probably the worst advice I could have or have ever been given. He essentially told me to have a stiff upper lip, to grin and bear it, to just get on with life otherwise I would find myself being controlled by panic attacks and I would eventually become unemployable. I was scared, confused and looking for help.

Instead I got, what became in my mind, a self-fulfilling prophesy!

That Counsellor gave me bad advice. I was too naive and trusting of advice that came from someone I thought knew what they were talking about. I really believed that I had to just try and struggle my way through this "setback" as he called it. I had to "grow up" and "stop being a coward". Yup he said those things too.

As you can imagine my self esteem hit rock bottom, I began to believe that I was going to end up as unemployable, unwanted. I began to believe I was going to panic for the rest of my life. I was scared.

I went back to work the next day and the next, but the attacks still came, more and more frequently. The more I fought against them the harder it seemed to cope with them. As it became harder to cope I worried that I was going to become unable to hold down my job, so I panicked more, which led to more worry and more stress and my world and my life began to slowly crumble down around me.

Eventually I had a severe panic attack whilst at work one day. I completely freaked out, ran out of the building right in the middle of a normal working day and never went back. I called in sick, for weeks, in the end I couldn't face going back. I felt like there was no help for me. I couldn't find the help I needed and I quit. I quit my job but I think for a while I also quit trying. Trying to cope, trying to manage, in some sense I had given up on myself.

I spent the next two and a half years almost house bound. I would panic if I left the house, if I was on my own in the house, if the weather was terrible, if there was a power cut, if we had visitors, if the postman came early, if the postman didn't come at all...Basically I got really really good at panicking!

I honestly came to believe that my life was to be that of a recluse. Never to have a job, never to have friends or a relationship, never to live the life I expected to live, a normal one!

Over the following months and years many different doctors and other health professionals gave me wonderful and life changing help and advice. I learned not to judge the advice given to me, by that one early bad experience but it took time. I learned to trust that there was a possibility of my life changing, of getting what I thought of as "better" and of leading a "normal" life.

Now, I am a little, ok a lot, older. I've had some really good jobs, none of which I have left because of panic attacks, and I have had, and hope to continue to have a really fortunate and fulfilling life. I have a beautiful daughter, beautiful partner, a lovely home and a strong group of friends.

I'm very happy.

I've come to believe that everyone can achieve happiness, that everyone deserves happiness in their life and that, anyone, absolutely anyone can master their fears and anxieties that hinder their life.

There is no magic bullet and no secret formula or special pill to take. I believe it takes patience, some courage, and the real desire to change. But anyone can do it!

Ian Parks

This short book is my offering of help to you, my effort at providing a helping hand and giving someone who felt like I used to some hope, a sign that you are not alone and that things can be better.

I hope this helps you and I wish you every success.

1 WHAT ARE PANIC ATTACKS

A panic attack is an intense feeling of fear or impending doom. For me personally it's a deep empty feeling in the pit of my stomach combined with the almost uncontrollable urge to run away from where-ever I am. My arms and legs tingle and it feels like they aren't mine. A panic attack is very real and the fear is genuine. They can be very debilitating and life changing.

For most people panic attacks can strike at anytime but normally occur in times of stress or anxiety. A pattern can emerge that become almost habit like and as a result panic can become a major focal point in everyday life. In cases such as this, panic is generally referred to as a "Disorder".

In fact many people experience panic now and again and then forget all about it straight afterwards. That feeling when you think you've lost your house or car keys, or when the truck in front cuts in lane right in front of you and you have to break hard and swerve to avoid hitting it. That intense emotional rush that comes as a result of a nasty surprise or a shock or even finding yourself in a potentially dangerous situation. It really is a rational reaction for this type of situation. We are designed to feel afraid at times and it is a perfectly normal reaction when we feel we are at risk. Which is why for most people a panic attack will normally be over and gone in a few moments and then forgotten about quickly afterwards. A few short, fleeting moments of intense anxiety followed quickly by a strong sense of relief.

However, for some of us, the experience of panic is as more frequent occurrence and most often at times when it is completely irrational and unexpected to feel panic. During times when we would normally be expecting to relax such as when we are in bed trying to drift off to sleep or maybe when we are eating lunch or dinner. Maybe when we are about to go to the shops or during many other daily activities we normally just take for granted.

Personally, I could even experience panic just by thinking about panic! I became so sensitive to it, so fearful of it, that I gave it a type of power over me and an ability to control me. I basically became afraid of being afraid. Even reading the word panic on a page, or hearing someone else speaking it out loud. I was constantly on edge and constantly mentally checking my body for signs of an impending attack. This constant monitoring of the feelings and sensations in my body and the thoughts going through my mind was exhausting. No matter how long I slept or rested, I always felt tired.

You will have your own experiences and your own personal relationship with panic. These may be similar to mine or completely different. Panic attacks however, are all based on the same internal natural process and are all fundamentally the same. No matter what we panic about or how different your fears or concerns are to mine, the tools and techniques to overcome these attacks will help you and me, in fact they can help anyone.

The underlying basis of every panic attack is a natural and harmless reaction called the Flight or Fight response. Some scientists now call it the Flight, Fight or Freeze response but what ever the name is, it is the reaction our bodies have which acts as the foundation blocks for most panic attacks.

Imagine you live in the middle of a deep tropical jungle and the probability of you bumping into a giant man eating tiger or tripping over a huge hungry toothy crocodile is fairly high. If this was the case the Flight or Fight response is a really useful and purposeful response. In fact it could save your life!

It sends surges of adrenalin through your body and prepares your muscles for quick and urgent action. Your nervous system fires up to red alert as your senses become hyper sensitive. It prepares your body for the struggle of your life! Your senses are alive and your muscles are tensed and ready to go!

But if you're brushing your teeth or bending down to tie your shoelaces, or even tucked up in bed and your body starts preparing for that epic Flight or Fight against a perceived threat it really isn't that helpful! It can be confusing and very frightening and upsetting.

It can also be completely debilitating as the Flight or Fight response triggers a set of chemical changes in your body which start to cause an immediate reaction in your nervous system and other bodily functions and senses and an increase in your body's readiness for some form of action.

These chemical changes, and the results of them are the physical symptoms we feel and associate with panic such as:

-Increased heart rate

-Palpitations

-Increased breathing rate

-Shortness of breath

-Shaking

-Feeling like you have lost control

-Changes to your body temperature

-Sweating

-Flushes

-Changes to your digestive system

-Butterflies in your tummy

-The need to go to the toilet

-Cramps

You might even find that you also experience tunnel vision and/or a loss of hearing as the pupils in your eyes dilate and your hearing functions close down temporarily, but these are more rarely experienced.

Now, and this is the really important and key point, as unpleasant and horrible as the panic which can stem from the Flight or Fight response is, it is, vital, to keep in mind that the underlying physical symptoms and emotions are natural, normal and harmless. The timing is always lousy and the trigger point may be irrational. Let's face it a panic attack is about as much fun as a rectal exam, but a panic attack is not going to do you any harm! It's very unpleasant but it will not kill you.

I have had too many panic attacks to count, but I'm still here and I have never, ever, came to any harm because of a panic attack. Sure I've got a bit sweaty, I've felt a bit dizzy and I've thought I was about to pass out. But I am still here, and so are you!

No matter how bad you feel, how frightened you are, you will always come out the other side of a panic attack. Always! Never forget that.

Think about this. Sportsmen and sportswomen train their bodies to the point where they can, when needed, run faster, jump higher or be stronger than their opponents. The physical feelings and reactions at the point of action, the height of their physical exertion, when competing against their opponents are very often largely the same as those in my body and your body when we are going through the Flight or fight response. The adrenaline rush, the tensed muscles, the increased heart rate.

Consider the many people that visit theme parks and fun fairs to experience and to enjoy strong feelings exactly the same as a panic attack on a roller coaster or a ghost train and they do this all for the sake of entertainment! The same applies to scary movies and even Halloween! Some of us are entertained by feeling afraid.

The difference though, I believe, is knowledge.

If you make a decision to watch a scary movie or to ride on a roller coaster you know what you are exposing yourself to. You expect to have weird feelings in your body and you expect to experience that thrill and fear for a short period of time. During that experience you know and understand absolutely why you feel this way, you want to feel this way and you know that once the ride stops or the movie ends, so will the feelings.

During a panic attack, when you may not even know why you are panicking, it might not even cross your mind that the experience is only temporary.

It is. Temporary and harmless.

2 IT'S A VICIOUS CYCLE

We experience the physical symptoms, we feel the fear and we go through the thought routines that are particular to us and our own panic attacks. I wonder how many of us actually understand what our body is going through during a panic attack. I wonder how many of us really know that it is a circular process or reaction. How many of us understand that it is a harmless and temporary process which is completely natural that has protected human beings and other types of animals from harm for, well for ever.

For me personally I found that knowing what my body was doing and why I was feeling the way I did during a panic attack, helped me understand what I was experiencing during an attack, and that understanding helped me begin to reduce the fear. Understanding what was happening allowed me to set aside those extra unrealistic fears and unhelpful thoughts that added to and prolonged the attack. This understanding helped me learn how to break the process and begin to shorten the length of attacks I suffered. I really believe that developing a complete understanding of your own panic "cycle" is one of the key tools in breaking free from panic.

Imagine your body as a natural system. A panic attack is a chain reaction and once the reaction starts your "system" responds as it is designed to do and the Flight or Fight response kicks into action. This is part of a chain reaction, a circular process which re-enforces itself as it progresses through each stage.

You may find that you are anxious or having a panic attack and that this can feel like you are at any part or stage of the panic cycle with no real understanding of what started it all off in the first place. I describe the chain reaction next but please remember that although I talk of a trigger you won't always feel like the process has such a defined starting point. I used to wake up panicking, noticing the feelings in my body with no clue what had happened to make me feel this way! The most important thing to remember is that the process can be broken at any point.

The Trigger.

There is always a trigger. Even if you don't know what it is. A feeling. A thought or an occurrence outside your body or something within. If, like me, you have already become really good at panicking you'll probably have become so used to finding yourself trapped inside the vicious cycle that you may often notice yourself there without having any real conscious or clear understanding of why you are anxious or panicking.

This is incredibly frustrating and frightening and it leads to the thinking and belief that a panic attack can strike without any warning. This can make us feel like we are out of control or at the mercy of something outside of ourselves. By learning about the vicious cycle and mastering the techniques for breaking it we can begin to take back and reassert that control and begin to believe again that our reactions are controlled by us, and not just something we have to suffer through or put up with.

Some people may find that they scan or monitor their body looking for signs of stress or anxiety and begin to question how they feel, "What was that twinge I felt? Am I ill? Is my heart ok? Am I feeling nervous? Am I going to panic?" Everyone will have a variety of questions like this that allow and encourage their panic to build.

The Feelings

Your heart rate or your skin temperature increasing. A sick feeling in the pit of your stomach. Pin and needles in your limbs. Many different feelings or symptoms exist that are linked to a panic attack and you may experience some, or all or different symptoms during different attacks.

These feelings cause alarm and cause the sufferer to imagine and question their nature about what they are or how severe or dangerous these feelings may be.

This leads to

The Thoughts.

The fearful or anxious thoughts, the negative, the worrying, the doubts and the what ifs? These thoughts build tension within you. This was the point at which I use to try really hard not to think about panic. Can you guess what that got me thinking about!

These thoughts are normally unrealistic exaggerations or negatively framed and very difficult to ignore. These thoughts begin and the panic becomes reinforced, and then you notice again stronger feelings or sensations in your body.

And then back to the beginning again...

So as you notice these stronger feelings, you go on to reinforce them with more irrational or unrealistic thinking, "Something's wrong" or "something's going to go wrong", "I'm having a heart attack", "I have to get out" are all common thoughts. These thoughts again cause the feelings within your body "the panic" to build and become stronger which in turn feeds your negative thoughts, which in turn feeds the physical sensations and the process goes round and around.

It truly is a vicious cycle but the good news is that you can break it!

The next time you experience an attack remind yourself that it is a natural process. That it is a chain reaction your body is going through and that it will get through. Remind yourself that it will be a temporary and harmless experience and although it is very frightening you are not in any danger. It may be happening at an irrational time but the fight or flight process is a reaction that has been designed into your body as mechanism to enable you to better protect yourself.

Try to notice the different parts of the cycle as your body and mind experience them. As you notice and recognise them, identify them to yourself. Try to become more aware of the thought part of the cycle and try to question how realistic those thoughts really are. Write them down. Aim to learn as much as you can about your panic attacks, the feelings and sensations you experience during them. When they happen, what you are doing, how they build and what thoughts you have during them, what physical symptoms you experience and the length of time they last.

Notice and learn as much about them as you can. Become an expert on your own particular brand of panic attack. Educate yourself about your panic until it almost becomes boring and mundane. Make a real effort to keep a panic diary, I will discuss this later, with all these details in it.

Notice carefully how you continue to not die because of these attacks!

If you have not done so already think about going to seek some medical advice from your Doctor. Sometimes panic attacks can also be caused or made worse by an underlying medical condition so it is worth getting this checked out. While you are there ask your Doctor to explain what a panic attack is, what the fight or flight response is and whether there is any possible harm that a panic attack could cause. Ask all the questions you have that you would like answered! Make a list of question before you go.

But try to reassure yourself that no matter how bad, how awful it feels to suffer a panic attack, no matter how fearful and traumatic it feels inside your body, the outside world is still, and will continue to, carrying on regardless. The clouds will still pass overhead, birds will still sing in the trees and the sun will keep shining.

The important point is that the world will not come to an end because of a panic attack, regardless of how many of those

"What if?" questions you manage to squeeze into and through your brain when you're feeling anxious or panicking!

If you need to be convinced, just look back over your own experience of panic attacks. Or think about the number of people in the world and the huge number of panic attacks that must have occurred over the entire history of the planet so far.

Has the world stopped, even once, because of them? No!

Don't allow yourself to pay too much attention to the fearful voice in your head trying to convince you otherwise. Be as honest with yourself about what is actually, really happening as you can be. I know it's not easy but it will really help.

3 IN AN IDEAL WORLD

What's the quickest way to stop worrying?

Simple, just stop worrying!

Frustratingly, we all know it's not that easy and I can imagine that if I was standing close to you right now you might want to punch me in the head for writing something so stupid and unhelpful.

I remember friends and family giving me similar advice and platitudes, caring, helpful people only wanting to make me feel better and I wanted to punch them in the head for not understanding how bad I felt and how out of control I was. I used to become really angry that some people thought that the solution was as simple as just not worrying about it

However, it is something to remember and keep in mind. I used to add to my panic because I worried about panicking! So I used to panic about panicking! It really was a very efficient process and if panic had been a product that could be packaged I would have been a world class manufacturing operation!

I used to create panic. Even now that is hard to write down. It is hard to understand and hard to accept but it is true. I created panic. It became a habit.

Once I learned to, and started to, trust myself and to accept that even if I did panic I would cope with the attack and get through it, the panic attacks started to shorten in length and then diminish in strength. Once I learned and began to accept that panic was not something that I needed to fear I felt a belief building in myself that I could cope.

An often used quote goes like this, "The only thing we have to fear is fear itself". I think this was said by Franklin D Roosevelt, but whoever said it had a moment of pure genius! Think about that quote for a moment. In terms of a panic attack the worst that can really happen is that you'll have a panic attack!.

So when we are panicking that really is as bad as it gets. We have done it before and most likely we will do it again but that is all it will be, a panic attack. Something that is temporary and harmless. Unpleasant yes, but temporary and harmless.

All of the unhelpful and irrational thoughts that fill up our heads when we are anxious, telling us we are going to die, or going to have to run away or going to have a heart attack or whatever, feel free to insert your own particular irrational thought here! All of these thoughts make us believe that something life threatening or tremendously bad is going to happen. The reality is that we are having a panic attack, nothing harmful is going to happen to us and it will pass.

This book will introduce you to the tools that can help you cope before, during and after any panic attack and then begin to actively reduce the impact that panic has on your life.

Guess what happens when you stop being afraid of having a panic attack? That's right, their power over you diminishes!

A Challenge!

From now on try to think of any panic attack you may have as an opportunity to try out the tools, methods and ideas you pick up from this book. Now I know you're never going to look forward to a panic attack but really try to think of the next attack as a chance to test out what you are learning. A training session for your new confident self.

These tools DO work.

I know because they have worked for me and they work for thousands of people every day. They don't always work first time but with persistence and a real desire to change they will work.

I know you have a desire to change as you wouldn't be reading this otherwise!

Anything we learn needs to be practised before we can become good at it. The same applies to the methods and tools in this book. However there is something that you have to be totally honest about with yourself before we make a start. Something you may find hard to admit to others but even harder to admit to yourself.

A panic attack creates fear and this fear creates a need in us, a desire in us to feel safe. It is often the case that because of our experience with panic we get used to being treated with great concern and care by others. We can become used to people making accommodations or exceptions for us. We get used to living our lives in a fashion that is designed to avoid situations and experiences where we might experience panic and in most circumstances others just have to fit in. In short, we have created our own little comfort zone.

We are going to have to accept that this comfort zone exists. We have to accept that we have created it because we needed it to help us cope. However, now we have to accept that this comfort zone has become an anchor which is, in reality, holding us back. It is preventing us from committing to getting better. There is a part of us inside that does not want to let go of the safety of this comfort zone. This part must be acknowledged and recognised.

If you do not recognise and accept this part of your own persona then it will work against you. It will be harder to believe in the advances you make using the tools that you learn, it will be harder to cast off the doubt that the tools are working, and cast off the doubts that the benefits you feel are going to last.

If you are committed to staying inside your safety zone then you will most likely have a fundamental view that nothing is going to make a big enough change in your life to make the panic attacks better.

I was the same. Someone would suggest a tool to help and my first reaction would be to look for reasons why it would not work. I wasted years of my life looking for reasons that these tools would not help. I regret that I wasted too much time before I just admitted that I was afraid of letting go and stepping outside of my comfort zone and gave myself an honest and genuine chance to get better.

When I did step outside I found that people still loved me as much as ever. They were even more supportive than ever as they could see the efforts I was making to help myself. When I stepped outside my comfort zone I found that I was stronger than I had ever thought. I was able to cope with and deal with so much more than I had imagined.

Right now you are probably not aware of how strong you are. You have probably lost belief in your own inner strength. But that inner strength is there and like any strength it needs exercise and use to become more and more powerful.

You need to give yourself permission to feel better.

4 BREAKING THE CYCLE

The following three chapters will describe some tips and tools that I use to break various points on the vicious cycle of panic.

These tips and tools can be used on their own or in conjunction with each other. You can and should adapt them to suit you.

I have included tools in the relevant sections as they make sense to me but you may find that some tools help you to relax more in a different type of situation than I describe. That is ok. If it works then go with it!

What you will need to do, without any doubt is persevere. Try, try and try again as the famous saying goes. Most of the tools will take practise and therefore you will need to work at them a few times before beginning to feel any lasting benefit.

However please do NOT allow those nagging doubts, which I know will creep into your mind, to undermine the efforts you make. Work at it and keep working at it.

It is worth it!

5 BREAKING THE CYCLE
THE TRIGGER POINT

The trigger point itself is not something we can always prevent.

Sure, we can easily avoid man eating tigers by never venturing into the jungle but our trigger points are not all external. We have to accept that sometimes we will become anxious or find ourselves in a stressful situation. We have to accept that our thoughts might wander and we may trigger our own anxiety at times. Everyone does this from time to time. Everyone has worries about something or other. Having trigger points is not the issue. How we react to those triggers is.

We will deal with better ways to react in the following chapters. However, for now I want to introduce you to something called the Stimulus Gap.

If we were to try and draw out or write down how we basically react to trigger points, we could create a very simple diagram or formula like this

Stimulus=Response

Do you know what stimulus triggers your panic response? Is it a thought? A feeling?

If you can find ways to notice and recognise the triggers of your panic attacks, you can then begin to find ways to increase the length of time you take to react to those trigger points. The longer this time is, the more able you will be to choose a rational reaction to the trigger point.

The time, more of a pause really, that sits in between the trigger and your subsequent reaction is called the Stimulus Gap.

It works in the same way if you, for example, find you loose your temper easily. You can learn to notice the fact that you are beginning to become angry and then, instead of boiling over into a rage straight away, you learn to consider why you are getting angry and if it is right to be angry at that time and basically give yourself a chance to choose your response in a more rational manner.

Or if you find yourself becoming very sensitive to the comments of others, again you can find ways to take time to consider what really was said, how it was said, who said it and what they really meant. Was the comment really intended to hurt your feelings or are you taking what was said in the wrong way?

The simple diagram or formula for this would now look like this

Stimulus = (GAP) response

This gap is the key as it allows you to think through and consider all of the possible options for a suitable response. It gives you the time and power to choose your reaction rather than react in the usual way. It allows you to consider your response or even ask a few questions before reacting. Adding this level of choice back into the situation gives you back a measure of control.

I think it is important that we understand two points here.

We need to learn to recognise and notice our trigger points and we need to learn how to give ourselves time to think through and choose alternative responses to the trigger points we experience.

How can you recognise the trigger points?

Ok I know what your probably thinking, sometimes I just panic! There is no trigger point, it just happens! I understand this, I used to feel the same way too. One minute nothing, next minute panic stations.

However there is always a trigger. It can be very subtle and it can be very quick but it will be there somewhere.

Remember the Panic Diary I mentioned earlier? Keep one! Sensing or recognising the triggers for your panic may not be easy to start with but this diary will help you to examine and review events and your responses.

Your Panic Diary should track your anxiety and panic levels throughout each day.

Find a note book or some paper. Each time you experience anxiety or a panic attack record the following

When - what time is it when you panic?

Where - where are you when you panic?

Why - What were you thinking about?

Why - What were you doing?

Level - How strong was your panic 1-10 (1 lowest to 10 strongest)

Level - How long did your panic last

Thoughts - What thoughts are going through your mind? (It is really important to do this as thoroughly as possible and to record your thoughts exactly as you frame them in your mind - If you think "I'm going to have a heart attack" then that is what you need to write down.

Review your diary as part of your learning about your own panic attacks. Do you notice any recurring themes?

Are there specific times of the day, places or thoughts that trigger your panic?

Over time you will be able to pick up a pattern and reveal the triggers. You will be beginning to build knowledge about your panic attacks and what triggers you are sensitive to.

The following chapters will give you tools to help you increase your stimulus gap.

6 BREAKING THE CYCLE
THE THOUGHTS STAGE

Tools for breaking the panic cycle at the thoughts stage.

We know that just thinking or worrying about a panic attack can actually trigger an attack. Our anxiety leads to what's often called "all or nothing" thinking. Your brain just seems to want to function in only black and white terms. Yes or no, on or off, right or wrong. It's almost as if it has shut down all of the clever parts of itself and it is only allowing access to the very simplest part. It feels like you cannot control how or what you think.

However consider this. If you can create panic just by thinking in a certain way, then the reality of it must be that you can also reduce and conquer panic also just by thinking in a certain way! If you can switch it on using just your own thoughts you must therefore be able to switch if off in the same way.

I have to admit I used to really REALLY struggle with this concept at first. It sounds too simple and too easy! Somehow it seemed just too simplistic for the horrendous ordeal I was going through every time I had a panic attack. Eventually I was persuaded that it was true. However no matter how hard I tried I could not seem to control my thoughts! No matter how much effort or how much fight I put into it, I just could not stop thinking about panic. So I learned to look at it differently.

Try this...Close your eye for ten seconds and do NOT think about different types of fruit.

What happened? Did you manage not to think about fruit?

Or did images of an apple, orange or banana pop into your head!

Maybe some grapes or a pineapple too.

The message here is that when we tell ourselves or try to force ourselves not to think about something we will only end up thinking about whatever that thing is even more!

So, instead of telling yourself not to think about panic or not to worry, instead of trying to fight off and ignore those thoughts, actually give yourself permission to think those thoughts. Don't try to fight them off, instead try to accept them.

You don't have to agree with them, you certainly don't have to believe those thoughts but just let them wander through your mind. Write them down in your panic diary and then examine them. Examine them and challenge them.

A really useful tool is a technique called "Alternative Thought"

You see, your brain is basically quite sneaky. It will pop thoughts into your consciousness that, at first, when you are in a panic state or becoming really tense might seem reasonable. So, if you're feeling really hot, sweaty and light headed you're brain might come up with something along the lines of "I'm going to pass out, fall over and hurt myself" or "I'm going to be really embarrassed, I'll never live this down". Sound familiar?

Take your version of those thoughts and write them down on a piece of paper. Then take time to review them and come up with an alternative version for each thought. What ever your "panic" thought is, don't try not to think it, instead try to examine it as realistically as possible and come up with a different set of words or a phrase which will more rationally and honestly describe the situation and how your are feeling. There are some examples below

Panic Thoughts	-	Alternative Thoughts
I'm going to pass out	-	I feel light headed so I'd like to find a chair and sit down.
I'm having a heart attack -		My heart is racing because I am anxious
I'm going to die	-	I feel awful, but it's just a panic attack.

Reframing your thoughts, which basically means putting them into a different perspective, and creating an "Alternative Thought" allows you to consider your feelings in a more balanced and realistic way. By challenging them like this you begin to reduce the impact that your thoughts have within the panic cycle.

Outcome Thinking

Like "Alternative Thought" this is a method of taking your original thought and changing how you express it to yourself. Many of us think constantly about what we don't want. We don't want to feel upset, we don't want to feel stressed, and we don't want to panic. Our brain reacts to these thoughts by focusing on exactly that, what we don't want! We then spend our time focused on the negative outcomes that we do not want to happen and feeling worn down by feeling like we are having a constant battle with our own thoughts.

A simple but effective change we can make is to change how we word our thoughts. Instead of consistently engaging in what is often called, "away from thinking", and thinking about what we do not want to happen, we can start to engage more in what is known as, "towards thinking" and thinking about the things we actually do want and the things we want to move towards.

Compare these two thoughts

I don't want to panic.

I would like to feel calmer.

Which one is more comfortable and relaxing?

The "I don't want to panic" thought leads me to think about panic. Exactly what I do not want. However by changing that original "away from thought" into a "towards thought" I end up working with a thought that helps me move towards how I actually want to feel.

Take some time and review your panic diary to see if there are any common thoughts that you have that could be changed from "away from" thinking into "towards" thinking.

If you have not started your diary yet just use a piece of paper to note down some frequent thoughts that you have and work with those instead.

One really important tip on using "Towards" thinking.

Do not put yourself under pressure by being over demanding in your thinking. Do not use phrases such as "I NEED to" or "I MUST". These are just another form of all or nothing thinking patterns and really don't help as essentially you are just giving yourself an instruction or an order but with no support to carry it out. By phrasing your thoughts like this you are setting yourself up to fail!

Instead try to use phrases such as " I would like to", "I would prefer to" or "It would be better if.." These are more open thoughts that do not add pressure to your situation and they are far more useful when dealing with anxiety and panic.

Combine Alternative Thought and Outcome Thinking to increase the benefits of the two techniques.

7 BREAKING THE CYCLE
THE FEELINGS STAGE

How to break the panic cycle at the feelings stage.

As we have discovered, the feelings you experience in your body during a panic attack lead to fearful and negative thinking. Which in turn leads to stronger sensations and feelings! However we can do something about those feelings and sensations as they happen and effectively reduce the impact and they have within the panic cycle.

The first and most important thing to understand and remember is this.

They are just feelings.

Like feeling too hot or too cold, like pins and needles, like goosebumps or a shiver down your spine. They are just feelings and they will not do you any harm now or in the future.

They are unpleasant, yes. They are unwanted, yes. Feelings can suck, yes.

But they are just feelings and you can do something to reduce them and bring them under control. The breathing and relaxation exercises below will help.

Breathing exercises

These work by slowing down and controlling your breathing. This prevents hyperventilation and helps to reduce the beating and pounding of your heart. By breathing in a calm measured way your body will begin to respond by relaxing. This will cause the feelings and sensations to decrease.

There are many different breathing exercises. The most important thing to remember with all of these is that, if the exercise feels like a strain or uncomfortable, then it is not going to help. If any of the breathing exercises in this book do not work for you, then adapt them to suit.

At first breathing in a different manner to what you are used to will feel a little strange. You may feel pins and needles like tingling in your arms and legs, this is normal and is caused by the oxygen levels increasing in your blood.

Read through each exercise and then give it a go.

With the following breathing exercises I recommend breathing in through the nose and out through the mouth. As you breathe out imagine stale and stressed air flowing out of you to be replaced as you breathe back in with cool and calming air. You can also try imagining the expelled air to be coloured red and the fresh incoming air to be a light calming green.

"The Three Count"

This is a classic breathing exercise. Simple, easy and effective.

Breathe in through your nose, slowly and deeply, but not forced, for a count of three.

(Make sure you breathe in only as slowly and as deeply as feels comfortable)

Hold for a count of three.

(Again it could be a count of two, or four. Whatever feels good)

Breathe out through your mouth, for a count of three.

(The aim is to create a slow, steady breathing pattern)

Hold for a count of three and then repeat.

Repeat the pattern for a couple of minutes.

As I mentioned you can adapt this exercise by reducing the count to two or increasing it to four or five. The holds in between each breath in and out can also be longer or shorter. They don't all have to be the same. However try to create a slow steady pattern. Increase the time you do this exercise for but never force it, it should be a relaxing experience.

"Push Up"

Lay flat on your back. Try to keep your muscles as relaxed and loose as possible.

Place your hands on your stomach. Just lay them one on top of the other, flat and relaxed, don't interlace your fingers or clench your fists.

As you breathe in through your nose (slow and regular breaths) notice how your belly pushes up.

(Now some of you will be trying this and thinking "My belly is going down as I breathe in!!", that's ok, you're not broken and you are doing it right it's just easier for some people to do this exercise the opposite way. So just follow the instructions but where I say "in and up" you'll actually be going "in and down")

As you breathe out (again slow and regular but not forced) feel your belly sink back down.

The pattern should be

Breathe in slow and steady - hold for a count of one - breathe out slow and steady - hold for a count of one - repeat.

Notice what your belly does as you breathe. As it moves slowly up and down try not to control it, just to let it just happen.

"The Bag"

A classic and probably the best known breathing exercise of all. Get yourself a paper bag. Now it doesn't have to be brown, I've checked, and white is ok but it can be whatever colour you like. Try not to use a bag from an old fast food meal, they really stink!

Hold it in one hand using your thumb and finger to form a sort of mouthpiece. Like the OK sign

Breathe slowly in and out of the bag. (Just using your mouth this time)

I have to be honest here; this one didn't work out for me. The first time I tried, I breathed out too hard and popped the bag! I nearly jumped out of my skin! Other people swear by it saying it is one of the most effective ways to calm down when you find you are panicking and your breathing rate is really high.

Try it to see if it works for you, but remember no fast food bags!

Relaxation Exercises

These exercises work by creating relaxation in your muscles and reducing tension in you muscles.

If you can it is easiest to do these exercises lying down but they can be done sitting down too. I'll describe them as if you will be lying down.

Another useful trick here is to combine the basic "Three Count" breathing exercise with each of these relaxation exercises for additional benefit.

Read through the exercises first, try to get them fairly clear in your head and then head for a quiet corner of your home.

"Tense and Relax"

Lie down on your back and close your eyes. Shrug your shoulders and hips to get as comfortable as possible.

Starting with your toes, as you breath in for a three count, clench your toes into a first as tight as you can. Hold it until its time to breathe out and then as you do breathe out release your toes from their first and feel the relaxation start to flow into them as the tension flows out.

Try imagining the tension flowing out in your exhaled breath.

Slowly and methodically work through the muscles in your body from toes right up to your shoulders and neck. Choose which ones you want to tense up and then relax. You don't have to work through every single muscle in your body, but as you do and each time you breath out, feel how the tension eases out of your muscles and the relaxation flows in to replace it.

You'll notice as you move up your body that the muscles you have already tensed and relaxed start to feel warm and heavy.

I used to work through the following muscles up to my neck

Toes

Calf muscles

Thigh muscles

Bottom muscles

Lower Back muscles

Stomach muscles

Upper Back muscles

Chest muscles

Firsts and forearms

Biceps

Shoulders

Once I reached my neck and head I would focus firstly on my jaw muscles and clench these tightly then release them as described before. I would purse my lips and push them together as hard as I could and then screw my eyes up then release and after each different clench and relax cycle I would enjoy the feeling of relaxation in my body as my muscles grew heavy and relaxed.

'

"Muscles Smile"

Another relaxation technique I found useful was the "muscle smile".

Essentially the same as the Clench and Relax but instead of clenching your muscles as you focus on different parts of your body, you visualise how the muscles are reacting to your relaxation.

So, again lay down in a safe quiet place. Again you can use the "The Count" breathing exercise if you wish.

Focus on your toes, but don't tense, instead inside your head tell yourself the following

"My toes are heavy and relaxed"

"My toes are warm and comfortable"

Again move through the different parts of your body and use this on each specific muscle group. Each time you repeat that you muscles are warm and comfortable visualise every cell in your muscle stretching it's arms out and yawning and smiling as all of the tension is released from it.

8 PREVENTATIVE MEDICINE

To deal with panic attacks effectively I strongly believe that there are some habits you can adopt which will greatly increase the benefits and effectiveness of all the techniques described in this book.

Now, please don't misunderstand me. I'm not going to tell you what you can eat or drink. I'm not going to tell you how much exercise you should have. Instead I'm going to tell you what works for me and make some suggestions about what I believe all of us should do. Especially if you want to do more to help yourself deal effectively with your panic attacks. I really think you should give serious consideration to the topics that follow in this chapter.

However, if you just want to concentrate on the techniques that directly focus on coping with panic attacks you can skip this chapter.

I'm going to talk about three things

Diet,

Exercise and

Relaxation.

As I said, if you want to, feel free to skip over this chapter and concentrate on the "Breaking the Cycle" and "Coping Strategies" chapters instead but please do think about coming back to this chapter at some time. I do think it will give you great benefit and it does form part of the "Routine for Change" chapter. But as I said, it is up to you.

Ok still with me?

I think how you treat your body is a great revealing factor in how you really feel about yourself as well as how you are feeling generally.

Do you respect your body?

Do you give it the proper nourishment and hydration it requires daily to function properly?

Do you eat regular meals?

Do you maintain a reasonable level of activity?

Do you make time to relax quietly and recharge?

If you do manage all of these things then please get in touch and let me know how you manage to squeeze it all in! Life is a busy place and we have so many demands on our time that it is really difficult to live the ideal lifestyle.

Actually I don't think it is possible to live the perfect lifestyle, so please do not take anything in this chapter as me telling you how to live your life. All I want to do is provide you with some ideas that may be of use to you. These are things that I have picked up or learned over the last twenty years. Some ideas here are just plain old fashion common sense but it is amazing how often we forget or ignore what we know as simple truths.

Diet

Not as in, "I must eat less!" or "I must lose weight!"

Actually look at those two statements and consider what you learned when we looked at in "Outcome Thinking". It really is not hard to see why lots of people find dieting so stressful considering how they often phrase their wants and desires in such all or nothing terms!

Anyway back to the point. By diet I just mean the food and drink we consume every day.

So thinking about your diet.

Are you a big coffee or tea drinker?

The amount of caffeine you are putting into your system every day can have a large contributory factor in anxiety levels? Did you know that caffeine is a stimulant, and that too much can make you more anxious. It certainly does for me.

I try to cut it out as much as possible but I do love a cup of hot sweet tea! I know that if I have too many cups I will get a caffeine rush. I know this will happen if I drink to much tea and I know that any nervous stimulation or extra anxiety will most likely be because of the caffeine.

I try to be as mindful as possible about how many cups of tea I have had. If I have too many I will feel like I am anxious but I can reassure myself with my "Alternative Thought" that it is just the caffeine in the tea that is stimulating my system. Nothing to worry about but it would probably be wise not to have another cup of tea for a while!

The same theory applies to sugary and fizzy drinks, they often contain caffeine or some other form of stimulant that provides the "boost" that their adverts love to boast about. Again I just try to be aware of when I have this type of drink. I very rarely take this type of drink in the evening or close to the time I go to bed.

Having said that another favourite drink of mine is a fizzy drink called Irn Bru. I never forbid myself having what I like, but I do make sure that I understand how the food and drink I have can affect my body and how I feel.

Chocolate has a reputation for being able to stimulate the feeling of love in the brain. However how many different ingredients or chemicals are contained within some chocolate, also in sugary sweets and candy. An old saying that is often quoted to me by my partner is, "a little of what you fancy" There is great wisdom in this. Eat and drink whatever you like but do so in moderation. Try to be as knowledgeable about what you are putting into your system, and how it can affect your system, as possible. If food or drink is going to have an effect on your body, I find it helps to know what it will be so that I can expect it and not be caught out. We all know what happens if we scoff down freezing ice cream, learn about the food and drink in your diet so that prevent other types of brain freezes!

I can also say, based on my own experience that, I feel much better eating fresh food, fruit and vegetables as often as possible, rather than having too many processed foods. If I eat too many burgers, frozen or microwave "ready" meals then I really notice a change in my energy levels and my quality of sleep. These two things for me have a huge impact on my anxiety levels.

However I also know that I love chocolate and if I deny myself that pleasure for too long it ticks me off!

So try to find a balance between eating and drinking what is good for you and indulging in what you enjoy.

Now please remember this is not a Diet Book, do not cut food or drink out of your diet completely that you enjoy! Do over do it either, just make sure that you try to eat as healthy and balanced a diet as you possibly can. If you do think that your diet may be playing a big part in your anxiety or panic then please go and talk to your Doctor. Get some professional nutritional advice.

As well as what, how you eat and drink is also a factor.

Do you rush your meals?

Do you chew your food enough?

Are you gulping your drinks?

I find that if I eat slowly, chew fully I better enjoy whatever it is. I was amazed and still am at how much of a difference this made for me.

I used to rush my meals, never chewing fully before forcing my food down and shovelling the next mouthful in. It was like a race and looking back I never enjoyed my food, never enjoyed the feelings I had in my body that were caused by how I ate. I usually felt bloated after my meals and often suffered from indigestion and heart burn and these feelings often led to panic!

By slowing down, chewing more and generally trying to enjoy my food I found I made a lasting difference to my anxiety levels.

Last points on diet (you'll be relieved to hear) is to consider when you eat.

I always try to avoid heavy meals in the hours before bed. (Unless I've been invited to a really nice restaurant!)

I also try to avoid alcohol and caffeinated drinks in the last few hours before I try to sleep. (most of the time!)

I make an effort to eat smaller meals more often, rather than large stuff-it-in till-I'm-full-and-ready-to-burst portions.

Exercise

Personally I used to find exercise to be a real bore. However that was when "I needed to get fitter". Note the unhelpful thinking there!

Instead, when I found that I really enjoyed going for a walk with my partner in the countryside, I realised that I was exercising but I wasn't putting myself under pressure to "get fit!"

I was told by my Doctor that the fitter your body is, the better it can deal with stress. He also quoted some figures from a study that showed how a certain level of exercise had the same benefits as a low dosage of antidepressant medicine. All very good but please do not just go out and start jogging! You will only end up with blisters and an aching body.

Find something to do that you enjoy. Something that can get you moving but that is not a chore, otherwise you will never keep it up!

It would be too easy to write about how many benefits exercise can bring. However we are not all sportswomen and sportsmen! Exercise to me means finding a way to be mobile. Walking to the local shop rather than driving, maybe taking the stairs rather than the elevator.

I do believe it is better to make an effort to exercise so please don't let me put you off a full blown fitness regime if that is what would work for you. We just need to each find something suitable and workable for us.

Regular relaxation

If you do something over and over you get really good at it. Relax regularly, get good at it. You will find that you can relax more quickly and more deeply each time. I really cannot recommend relaxation enough. It is something so simple, essentially sitting doing nothing, but it can have such a huge impact on how you feel. I think that once, at least, or preferably twice or even three times a day, its great to make some time and some space and give yourself five or ten minutes complete relaxation.

Use one of the exercises in this book. Maybe get yourself a CD with some relaxing music or even just read a book.

Time spent relaxing is often seen as a waste of time. You could be getting on with something productive! I used to feel guilty when I tried to relax. I used to feel like I was wasting time and that I should be doing something else. It took a while before I realised that it was actually ok, in fact it was completely reasonable, to give myself some time out to relax.

I found that after relaxing properly I could concentrate better. I was able to get even more done. I was much more effective in what I was doing. So I began to think about relaxing as something that I did to aide and improve myself and therefore definitely not something to feel guilty about.

9 RELAXTION EXERCISES

There are many ways people find to relax. Watching TV, playing sport or reading a book.

I find it really useful to make time just to switch of completely and do nothing but relax. To allow my body to release all of the tension it has stored up during the day and to let my mind forget all but the most basic thoughts.

This chapter details two fantastic relaxation exercises that I found particularly helpful in dealing with my panic attacks.

Muscular relaxation and deep breathing are the two most used methods to help aid relaxation. The following two exercises combine both. I still use these exercises today, most often last thing at night as I prepare for sleep. As I lie in bed I'll use one of these exercises to completely relax and unwind before I drift off. Most of the time I drift off before I get to the end of the exercise!

As with anything new these exercises need to be practised. You can adapt these easily to suit you and make them more personal. Use words that fit with you and mean more to you. These will be your relaxation exercises, so make them your own and they will help you more. You can if you wish, record yourself talking through these exercises onto tape, disc or even digitally if your technically minded. I find listening to them via headphones really adds to their effectiveness. You might feel a little self conscious listening to your own voice at first but you'll soon get used to it. If can you might even want to get someone else to record these for you!

Wear loose fitting clothes and make sure to take your shoes and socks off.

Find somewhere warm and comfortable to lie down, your bed or the sofa will do.

Try to arrange not to be disturbed.

The Stairs

Close your eyes.

Put your arms down by your sides, wriggle your fingers and toes and then settle in comfortably.

Begin to breathe slowly and deeply.

Feel your body being supported fully.

Begin by imagining nothing but the colour green. Let it be everything.

Whatever crosses your mind just turn it green. Pictures, words, sounds everything becomes green.

Breathe

Imagine yourself at the top of a wide stair case.

It is a beautiful day and the most gentle and warm breeze caresses your skin.

The stairs are strong, solid and safe.

A warm light shines down upon you and you begin to feel tension draining from your body.

There are ten stairs. Ten strong solid stairs which lead down to a beautiful garden.

Note **Pause between each stair and enjoy the sensations as your body relaxes.**

You take a slow deep breath, breathing in cool calming air.

You take a step forward and down onto the ninth stair.

As you pause, you breathe out slowly, feeling your body begin to relax as the tension flows from your body.

Breathing in again you prepare to step down onto the next stair.

As you step onto the eighth stair you feel your body become ten times more relaxed and your mood become ten times more serene.

As you breathe out your muscles become more and more relaxed.

You take another slow breath in, cool calming air filling your lungs.

As you step down once more you feel your body once again become ten times more relaxed.

You breathe out on the seventh stair and let your eyes wander to the beautiful garden below.

Your mood becomes ten times more serene and calm as you step down onto the sixth stair.

Your inward breath brings a flood of fresh calming air into your lungs.

Your muscles ease and release all tension as you breathe out.

Breathe in once more as you move downwards onto the fifth stair.

Every step downwards now is making your body feel ten times more relaxed, your thoughts ten times more serene

Pause for a moment now to notice how the feeling of relaxation is flowing through your body.

As you step onto the forth stair you body once again becomes ten times more relaxed

As you move closer to the garden now, breathing slowly and calmly, your muscles cannot help but become more and more relaxed.

Calm air flows gently into and out of your lungs as you step down once again onto the third stair.

Your muscles increase their relaxation more and more as the feeling of wellbeing becomes ten times stronger.

The second stair seems to pull you towards it now as you sink down towards the garden.

Your body feels like it is beginning to flow as your muscles again become ten times more relaxed.

Every breath now further increases the feelings of relaxation and wellbeing.

As you step onto the first and final stair you pause to enjoy the total relaxation flowing throughout your body.

Every breath continues to increases the feelings of calmness, relaxation and warmth.

Enjoy the relaxation and the warm calm feelings throughout your body

When you want to, step out into the beautiful garden, taking the relaxation and serenity with you.

Body Scan

Find a warm comfortable place where you will not be disturbed, preferably lying down.

Close your eyes.

Start with five complete breaths. Breathing in and out slowly and calmly.

Focus on your forehead. Notice how it feels.

Is your brow furrowed ?

Are your muscles tight?

Do you feel tension?

Notice any tension you feel in your forehead.

As you breathe out, release any tension from your forehead and feel your forehead relax.

Pause for a couple of slow calm breaths

Now focus around your eyes. Notice how they feel.

Are they tightly closed?

Do they feel tired?

Do they feel strained?

As you breathe out again release any tension from around your eyes.

Keep your breathing slow and calm, feel the air flowing into your nose and down deep into your lungs.

With each exhalation let go of tension.

Now focus on your mouth and jaw.

Notice any tension or stress that you have in the muscles around your mouth and along the bones of your jaw.

With an outward breath let your lower jaw bone drop slightly and your mouth open a little.

Release any tension completely from your mouth and jaw.

Breathe in and then out again releasing the tension.

Pause for one breath

Focus now on your neck and shoulders.

Shrug your shoulders slightly, notice the relaxation flow into your neck and shoulders as the tension releases with each exhale.

Now move your focus to your arms.

Can you feel any tension in your elbows, wrists or fingers?

Do you notice any tension or stress in these joints and the muscles around them?

Notice this clear as you feel the muscles in your arms and the palms of your hands down to your finger tips.

Feel your arms get heavy as they let go and relax

Notice your bed (or chair) beneath you.

Feel your weight supported by it.

Continue your slow breaths as your body grows heavy and more relaxed.

Now scan your upper and lower legs for tension or stress.

Breathe in and focus on this tension.

Breathe out slowly and completely.

As you next breathe in release all of the tension and stress that you have stored in your legs.

Breathe out and let your legs feel heavy against your bed.

Breathe.

Focus again on your forehead, eyes, mouth and jaw.

If any tension has slipped back into these areas, just use your deep slow outward breaths to release it and let go.

Breathe.

10 QUICK SUGGESTIONS

People often think that they can't cope. Very often people actually say they can't cope!

But we do! We cope.

It would actually be much more accurate to think and say something along the lines of, "I'm bored of just coping, I want to start enjoying!"

To start enjoying we need to find ways to make coping a little easier. The techniques that I have described already in this book will work for you and help you to move from feeling like you are coping to feeling that you are enjoying. They will help you regain control of your feelings and they will enable a steady building of inner confidence. These techniques will do this but there are so many more.

There are books written solely on the "Alternative thought" technique, or solely on using breathing exercises. Instead on focusing on a single effective technique I've tried to give you access to a few different tools in a short, easy to digest book.

In this chapter I want to briefly suggest two other things to try.

Talking

Plain and simple. Just talk to someone

There are many thousands of people throughout the world who experience panic attacks. Probably more.

At some point each and every of us will feel like we are going mad or that we are helpless. We feel alone and desperate.

We now know these thoughts for what they are, just a negative manifestation of our anxiety creating all or nothing thinking, but sometimes panic is still a lonely place.

If you have not already please do tell someone about your panic attacks. A relative, a friend or your own Doctor. Please don't feel embarrassed or ashamed by how you feel. When I finally managed to discuss my panic attacks with a friend I was amazed to hear her telling me about the panic attacks that she had experienced! I've spoken with other friends who really could just not "get" why I was panicking. They did not get it but they were my friends and they wanted to be supportive. I explained to them as best I could what I felt and they tried to understand as best they could.

Once you talk to one person, it is much easier to talk to the next. You will at some point talk to people who do not understand but I guarantee that pretty soon you will find yourself talking to someone who has also experienced a panic attack. Someone with a similar experience to you, that can relate to how you feel, and possibly even someone who can help you or that you can help.

I spent too many years being embarrassed and feeling that I was weak. I was ashamed of my panic attacks and I did my best not to admit why I was not going to go to out for a drink or didn't want to go to see the latest movie. My friends must have thought I really didn't like them as I always found an excuse not to go along!

When I finally spoke up and explained what I was going through I felt such a feeling relief. No longer did I have to think up excuses and I didn't have to feel bad about not being honest with my friends.

"Focusing on right NOW"

This is a type of distraction technique which is made very powerful as you will distract yourself with the reality all around you.

Write the following on a piece of paper and keep it with you. When you feel anxious or panicky pull out the piece of paper, take a good look around you and answer the following questions.

What can you see right now?

What is happening around you right now?

What is the weather like right now?

What can you hear right now?

What can you smell right now?

Answer the questions as fully and as descriptively as you can.

For example if you can see a tree, don't just think I can see a tree! Think about how big it is? What colour are its leaves? What shape are its leaves? Have you ever seen a tree like this one before? Does it remind you of anything? Are there any birds in it? Are they singing? What else can you hear?

Focus strongly on Now, what is happening now, not what you think is going to happen in a little while, or what you are worried might happen later but the reality of what is going on now.

Look at the world, where ever you are right then and there (The NOW) and focus on it. Be as mindful of it all as you possibly can. You may even want to take a small note book with you and use it to jot down the things you see and notice, hear and smell.

Working with the reality of what is going on at that precise moment allows you to focus on the real and what actually is, rather than concentrating on what we imagine or fear may happen.

11 CHANGE

In previous chapters I have provided you with a range of ideas that can be used to help overcome panic attacks and anxiety. The most important point I want to get across at this point is that you cannot just read this book for those ideas to work. You have to put them into use.

I used to read books about panic attacks and dealing with fear and then wonder why I didn't feel any better afterwards. I was building a great knowledge base on the subject but I was doing nothing with it! I'd try a new exercise, maybe once or twice and then move impatiently on to look for the next quick cure. I had no tenacity and looking back I have to admit that the biggest hindrance for me in dealing successfully with panic attacks was me.

Absolutely hating the way I felt, I just wanted to be "normal" but I wanted it straight away! I did not want to suffer from panic attacks any more and I did not want to be afraid and I wanted to be better. Quite demanding really huh? But I was missing a crucial and fundamental point and this was preventing me from moving forward with my own healing.

Whilst I knew what I wanted, I did not understand that I had to go on a journey. I did not appreciate that the knowledge I was building was useless, unless I put it into practice. I had to take a step forwards and instead of just learning, I had to start applying.

The ideas in this book will help you. As long as you work with them and continue to work with them over time. You can't read a book about long distance running to prepare yourself for a marathon. You wouldn't read a book about slimming and then wonder why you had not instantly lost any weight. Similarly, the ideas in this book need your effort and commitment to be able to help you.

Change is often thought of as a difficult thing to achieve but our lives changes every day! Our bodies change, our opinions change and our outlooks change. Sometimes this change happens without our awareness. I remember waking up one day and wondering who this bald guy was looking back at me from my mirror! Sometimes the change is small and happens with our knowledge but without us thinking about it. We change our clothes, we don't eat the same things every day, and we use different products or go to different shops or restaurants.

Change happens. It is really not that difficult to achieve. The difficult part is accepting that you can change and then making a start. Making a start and keeping going.

I want you to make a start and I want you to keep going, and to achieve the changes that you would like for yourself.

The first step, always thought of as the hardest, is to accept that you have a choice.

That choice is to "Do nothing" or "Do something".

I want you to choose to do something. However that is and always will be your own decision. What I want you to do is irrelevant. What do you want to do?

What are you willing to do to achieve that change?

Thank You

In closing I'd like to thank you for reading this. I'm sure I could have done a better job of writing this and maybe have been clearer in some of my ideas but I hope that I have got across to you that your life need not be ruled by anxiety or panic attacks.

I really hope that you give the ideas in this book a try. Not just once! A proper and committed effort to achieve a positive change in your life.

I recommend you start with the panic diary if nothing else. Keeping a record of how you feel leading up to and during a panic attack, how many attacks you have etc really can provide you with invaluable information about what it really going on. I used to think that I constantly felt panicky. By keeping a panic diary I discovered that wasn't true and there were large parts of my day in which I felt fine. This knowledge really allowed me to put the panic attacks into proper perspective.

By writing this short book I wanted to help others to begin to help themselves. Some of the advice is fairly straightforward or maybe even blunt. But that's how I see it. I try hard not to regret the time I wasted by not choosing to do something. But it is hard and sometimes I do look back and think, if I had only just started earlier. Don't waste another moment!

I have a happy and productive and fulfilling life. It really is a fantastic life full of love and happiness. There are also hard times to, as for everyone there are always good days and bad days, but those bad days only make the happy times mean so much more.

Looking back at the end of each day, I hope that you can begin to say that today was a good day.

www.ingramcontent.com/pod-product-compliance
Lightning Source LLC
Chambersburg PA
CBHW071329310526
45789CB00017B/2139